INTR

This book is designed _____ _____ __ _____ ___
easy with a gourmet touch. Instead of using difficult recipes and special equipment, information will be centered on the basics. In doing so, electric appliances and exotic formulas are excluded for the most part. On the other hand, gas stoves, grills and campfire accessories will apply to nearly all topics. Even though some recipes call for different equipment not ordinarily used for campfire cooking, all outdoor cooking devices are considered related as far as campfire cooking is concerned.

Ingredients consist mostly of fresh meat, fish, canned goods and customary spices. This is solely to save time, while reducing clutter and making recipes as easy as possible. Some recipes call for fresh vegetables. Use them whenever you can. There's nothing that tastes or smells better than bacon, onions and potatoes cooked in the great outdoors.

Recipes often refer to a heat source as a flame. For example, "heat a 10 inch skillet over medium flame." This does not necessarily mean flames from a fire. Instead, it symbolizes using medium hot coals, charcoal, or flames from a gas grill.

Desserts, marinades, and spices are most often fixed at home. You may wonder then, why are these subjects listed in this book. These products play an important role in campfire cooking. Meat is rather bland without spices or marinades, and desserts are just plain fun. That is, if you don't mind watching the kids run around with mucky faces.

Campfire Cooking
...with a gourmet touch
Achieved With Ease
by Brad Probst

Without my mom (Donna Probst), this book wouldn't be possible. Recipes she got from her mom are consolidated into this book. So, as a family, we dedicate this book to Essie May Butler.

Essie May Butler
Sept. 13, 1887 - Oct. 13, 1987

PUBLISHED BY:
Rome Industries, Inc.
1703 W Detweiller Dr.
Peoria, IL 61615-1688
www.pieiron.com

Table of Contents

HELPFUL HINTS

MEAT PRODUCTS

Meat such as poultry, pork and beef should be cooked thoroughly. After cooking, if pink or bloody meat dominates the middle of this food, dangers of food poisoning are at risk. Hands should be washed with soap and water before and after handling these meat products. Most fish products don't need to be cooked. In fact, about the only dangers of eating fish, is freshness, or over exposure to long periods of non-refrigeration. (KEEP FISH FRESH AND ON ICE!) Most fish can be eaten raw. Warning: Parasites in raw fish, or under-cooked fish can cause tape worm. This Japanese dish is called sushi. If for some reason you decide to eat it this way, go ahead. I'm going to cook mine!

FISH PRODUCTS

Most fish products don't need to be cooked. In fact, about the only dangers of eating fish, is freshness, or over exposure to long periods of non-refrigeration. (KEEP FISH FRESH AND ON ICE!) Some fish can be eaten raw...*Warning:* Parasites in raw fish, or under-cooked fish can cause tape worm. This Japanese dish is called sushi. If for some reason you decide to eat it this way, go ahead. I'm going to cook mine!

VEGETABLES

Vegetables should be rinsed with cold water. Scientist have proven that washing of fruits and vegetables has little effect on salmonella, or other similar bacteria. However, if particles or pesticides are present, organic herbs must be rinsed. Another good reason for washing fruits and vegetables, you don't know who's grimy hands has handled them at the super market. On the other hand (so to speak), most cases of salmonella come from people not washing their own hands. Thick skinned fruits and vegetables such as cantaloupe and potatoes, should be rinsed under cold water while being brushed. Even though, intense heat will kill bacteria, you never know what these products have rolled around in. Note: To prevent E coli, wash all vegetables or fruit, and cook meat thoroughly.

Things to Remember

Camping is for fun, not work. These items will help you save time and make campsite chores simple and easier.

Plastic Coated Paper Plates
Prevents juices from soaking through, saves on cleanup.

Plastic Forks, Spoons & Knives
Discard for the sake of dish-pan-hands.

Plastic & Insulated Cups
Plastic for cold, insulated for hot.

Can Opener
Don't forget it!

Spatula & Tongs
Used to turn hot foods with.

Chopping Board
A place where fingers are easily cut off. BE CAREFUL!

Matches
Carry wherever you go.

Scouring Pad & Soap
For cleaning pots and pans.

Paper Towels
For wiping up spills, etc.

Gloves
Great for gathering firewood or removing hot pans.

Items Sometimes Forgotten		
Flashlight	Propane Stove	Food
Tent	Grill	Pots & Pans
Sleeping Bag	Charcoal	Ice Cooler
Sleeping Cot	Starter Fluid	Spices
Coat	Propane	Camera & Film

Chapter 1

Skillet Menus

A skillet is more commonly known as a frying-pan. Probably more vittles are cooked over a campfire this way than any other. Usually the skillet will be placed directly on a bed of hot flat coals, or 1–2 inches above. It is recommended not to use your best kitchen ware for cooking over campfires. Flames and hot coals will almost instantly turn your pots and pans black.

Most of the time a skillet is heated before adding oil, margarine or butter. This prevents oils from burning, and foods from sticking while rendering a robust flavor. During the process of cooking long meals or boiling water, hot coals tend to go cold. Be prepared, have extra kindling to stoke the fire with.

Fisherman's Casserole

Feeds 2 to 4 as dinner

catch of the day (fish)
1 package macaroni & cheese
1 10-ounce can, cream of mushroom soup
   margarine or butter

Most any kind of fish can be used. Two pan-sized trout, bass, pan-fish fillets, or a can of tuna fish is sufficient.

Heat 12 inch skillet over medium flame, until hot. Add 2 tablespoons butter and cook fish until done. Remove skin and bones and place meat between two paper plates.

Fill skillet, 3/4 full with water and bring to a boil. Stir in macaroni and boil for 7 minutes, or until noodles are tender; stir occasionally. Drain water from skillet, then stir in packaged cheese, fish and cream of mushroom soup. Cook over medium flame for about 5 minutes until hot; occasionally stirring.

OPTION: Take 1 cup of crushed potato chips and sprinkle a thin layer over top of casserole.

Pan-Fried Perch

Feeds 4 to 6 as dinner

1 1/2 pounds perch, fillet
1 large egg
1/2 cup flour or corn meal
vegetable oil

Heat vegetable oil (1/8 inch) in 10 inch skillet over medium flame.

Beat egg with 1 tablespoon water, until blended. Dip fillets into egg, then coat with flour. Place fillets in skillet and sprinkle moderately with cajun spice and lemon pepper. Fry fish in hot oil, 6–10 minutes while only turning once. Fillets should be a medium dark brown on both sides when done.

Place fillets on paper towel to dry.

OPTIONS: This plate is excellent served with the Shredded Potato Melt meal (page 19), or the Golden Nugget Supreme (page 22).

Landslide Lasagna

Feeds 4 as dinner

1 pound ground beef
1 medium onion, chopped
1 medium green bell pepper, chopped
3 cups mini lasagna noodles, uncooked
1 30-ounce can spaghetti sauce
1 small jar sliced mushrooms

Cook beef, onion and bell pepper in 12 inch skillet over medium flame about 6 minutes. Stir occasionally until beef is brown, then drain off excess fat. Stir in 2 1/2 cups of water and remaining ingredients; bring to a boil. Reduce flame to simmer and cook 10–12 minutes, or until pasta is tender. Stir occasionally while cooking.

This dish may look like a landslide, but it tastes a whole lot better than it looks.

"Work around the campsite is something nobody notices, unless it doesn't get done."

Trapper Jim's Goulash

Feeds 4 as dinner

1 1/2 pounds boneless chuck, tip or round roast
1 cup beef broth
3 large onions, chopped
1 8-ounce can whole tomatoes
3 tablespoons paprika
2 cups elbow noodles, uncooked

Cut beef into 3/4 inch chunks. Heat 1 tablespoon vegetable oil in 12 inch skillet over medium flame. Place beef in skillet and stir occasionally while cooking about 15 minutes, or until beef is brown; drain oil. Stir in broth, onions, paprika and tomatoes (breaking tomatoes up), then bring to a boil. Reduce heat to simmer, cover and cook about 75 minutes or until beef is tender.

Boil elbow noodles 8–10 minutes, or until tender. Serve beef mix over noodles.

Great recipe for sitting around the campfire!

Pork Chop Bog

Feeds 4 as dinner

4 pork chops
1 10-ounce can cream of mushroom soup
1 1/2 cups milk

Salt and pepper chops to taste. Brown chops in deep 12 inch skillet over medium flame; drain fat.

Mix cream of mushroom soup and milk together and pour over chops. Cover skillet with lid and simmer 1 hour. (Turn chops over and stir mushroom mix after 30 minutes.)

Serve with instant mashed potatoes. Pour existing mushroom mix over potatoes and chops.

Conventional Oven
Bake in deep covered dish 1 hour
at 375 degrees after browning.

"Forgive thine enemies, There's nothing that ticks them more."

Bum Beef Casserole

Feeds 4 as dinner

1 pound ground beef
1 package macaroni & cheese
1 10-ounce can cream of mushroom soup
2/3 cup milk

Chop beef up with spatula in deep 12 inch skillet, and season with salt and pepper to taste. Cook over medium flame while occasionally and stirring and chopping. Prepare macaroni & cheese as directed on package.

When beef is done, stir in all ingredients. Cover skillet, cook about 10 minutes over medium flame while occasionally stirring.

The Hobo

Some call me homeless,
others relate me to dirt.
The world scolds me as scum,
a few say I'm allergic to work.
I'm not one to complain,
I lay around all day,
Sitting under a shade tree,
or watching my fire play.
I get up in the morning,
I go to bed at night.
I observe snarling humanity,
wondering what's wrong or right.
So, if congestion and confusion,
is where you come from.
All I ask of you is,
please don't call me a bum.

Steak & Potato Man

Feeds 4 as dinner

2 pounds round steak, cut into bite-size pieces
1 15-ounce can whole potatoes, chopped
1 15-ounce can green beans, whole
4 strips bacon, cut into squares
1 small onion, chopped

Cut away all fat and gristle from steak. Cook steak over gas or campfire grill, until done.

Cook bacon and onion in 12 inch skillet over medium flame, until done.

Drain water from potatoes and green beans. Stir in bite-size pieces of steak and remaining ingredients. Season with black pepper to taste. Cover skillet, cook about 10 minutes over medium flame while occasionally stirring.

Everyone will indulge in this delicious meal, and it will especially satisfy the steak and potato man.

Cowboy Delight

Feeds 4 as dinner

1 1/2 pounds ground beef or 1 pound. bacon
1 onion, diced
1 green bell pepper, chopped
1 30-ounce can stewed tomatoes
1 cup salad macaroni noodles, uncooked

Chop beef up in deep 12 inch skillet, salt and pepper to taste. Cook beef, bell pepper and onion over medium flame until beef is brown; drain fat. Stir in tomatoes and bring to a boil. Add macaroni and 2 heaping tablespoons of sugar, then stir.   Cover skillet, simmer for 20–30 minutes, or until macaroni is tender.

While cooking food, stir every 5–10 minutes with spatula so noodles don't stick to the bottom. Add water if needed to boil macaroni. If meal is to watery, leave lid off and cook down.

OPTIONS: Some people prefer bacon instead of beef. Either one is excellent. Just cut bacon into 1 inch squares and cook until brown. Follow directions to recipe above.

Cutthroat Scampi

trout (cutthroat, brook, or rainbow)
1/2–2 pounds
margarine (squeeze bottle type)

Fillet fish and season heavily with your favorite spice. Cajun, lemon pepper or garlic salt works great. If whole trout is used, cut off head, tail and fins, then season heavily inside and out.

Heat 12 inch skillet over medium flame, until hot. Fill skillet 1/8 inch with margarine. Place fish in skillet and squeeze a zigzag line of margarine along top of fish. Cook trout over medium high flame 10–15 minutes, while occasionally turning. Trout should flake apart with fork when done. Larger trout will take longer to cook.

OPTION: Serve with boiled, buttered rice; "yummy."

Jeff Probst
landing a
cutthroat
at
Yellowstone Lake

Cattle Rustlers Stew

Feeds 4 as dinner

1 pound boneless beef chuck, tip or round roast
1 large potato, cut into 1 inch chunks
2 medium carrots, cut into 1 inch chunks
1 small onion, chopped
1 green bell pepper, cut into 1 inch pieces

Cut beef into 1 inch chunks. Heat 1 tablespoon vegetable oil in 12 inch skillet over medium flame. Place beef in skillet and stir occasionally while cooking about 15 minutes, until beef is brown. Add 3 cups hot water, bell pepper and a dash of salt; bring to a boil. Reduce heat to simmer, cover skillet and cook for 2–2 1/2 hours, or until meat is tender.

Stir in remaining ingredients. Cover skillet and cook 30 minutes, or until vegetables are tender. Salt and pepper to taste.

OPTIONS: Other vegetables can be thrown into the stew such as celery, turnips, or whatever you can rustle up.

Trekkers Trout Helper

Feeds 2 to 4 as dinner

2–3 pan-sized trout, skinned & boned
1 package Tuna Helper®
margarine or butter

Heat butter in 12 inch skillet over medium flame until hot. Cook fish until done. Skin and bone trout and place between two paper plates to keep warm.

Fill 12 inch skillet 3/4 full with water and bring to a boil. Stir in Tuna Helper and boil moderately for 8–10 minutes, or until noodles are tender; stir occasionally.

Drain off water and add 2 tablespoons butter, contents of package seasoning and fish. Cook for about 5 minutes over medium flame while occasionally stirring.

TIP: Covering skillet with lid will help water boil more rapidly, especially at high altitude.

"A fish tale won't make the meal any bigger."

Bootleg Egg Souffle

Feeds 4 for breakfast

6 large eggs, whipped
8 strips bacon
5 medium green onions, sliced
1/3 cup milk
butter

Cook bacon in 10 inch skillet over medium flame, until crisp. Place bacon on paper towel to drain.

Mix eggs and milk together with a pinch of salt and pepper, then whip with a fork.

Heat a couple tablespoons of butter in 10 inch skillet over medium flame. Pour egg mix into skillet and cook 3–4 minutes, or until eggs have thickened but still moist. Crumble bacon strips, then sprinkle bacon bits and green onions on top. Lift souffle around edges so uncooked portions can flow to the bottom to cook. When moisture has dissipated, souffle is done.

This dish may not resemble a souffle. But then bootleggers are known to make one product and call it something else. Anyhow, this is how I would like to think a bootlegger would brew up a souffle.

Shredded Potato Melt

Feeds 6 to 8 as side dish

6 medium potatoes, peeled and shredded
1 10-ounce cream of chicken soup
1/2 pint sour cream
1 cup cheddar cheese, grated
1/4 cup butter
1 tablespoon dehydrated onion

Peel potatoes, cut in half and boil for 20 minutes; then shred.

Heat 12 inch skillet over medium flame and spray with cooking oil. Place potatoes, soup, sour cream, dehydrated onion and 2/3 cup cheese into skillet and stir. Pour melted butter over mixture, and layer the rest of grated cheese on top. Cook over medium flame for 20 minutes, or until cheese has melted.

Conventional oven:
Use 1 large package of frozen hash browns, instead of potatoes. Bake in deep covered dish at 350 degrees for 30 minutes.

"Behind-the-back words are bad decision, for tomorrow you may have to eat those conniving words of wisdom."

Backpacker's Pledge

Off in the woods I go,
with my home strapped to my back.
  I leave my worries behind,
and that's a natural fact.
  The wilderness is a friend of mine,
it really is a beautiful place.
  Animals can be heard here and there,
and sometimes show their face.
  If I said I'd be home real soon,
it probably was a lie.
  I would rather fish all day,
than sit at home and die.

by Brad Probst

Jeff at Red Knob Pass,
High Uinta Mountains

Huevos Rancheros

Feeds 6 for breakfast

1/2 pound pork sausage
1 1/4 cup tomato salsa
6 large eggs
6 corn tortillas
1 1/2 cups shredded cheddar cheese
vegetable oil

Cook sausage in 8 inch skillet over medium heat until done. Drain off fat, and cover to keep warm.

Heat (1/8 inch oil) in skillet over medium flame. Cook tortillas in oil, one at a time for 1 minute, while turning once. Tortillas should be crisp when done.

Heat salsa in 1 quart sauce pan while occasionally stirring, until hot.

Fry eggs in skillet, over easy, or your choice.

Spread each tortilla with 1 tablespoon salsa. Place 1 egg on each tortilla and top with salsa, sausage and shredded cheese.

Golden Nugget Supreme

Feeds 4 to 6 as side dish

1 15-ounce can whole kernel corn
1 15-ounce can whole potatoes, chopped
1 medium onion, chopped
1/2 pound bacon, cut into 1 inch squares
1 4-ounce can whole mushrooms

Cook bacon and onion in 12 inch skillet over low flame, until done. Drain excess fat from skillet, but leave a little to cook with. Stir in potatoes and sprinkle with black pepper and lemon pepper to taste. Cover skillet, cook over medium flame while periodically turning with a spatula.

Drain water from can of corn and mushrooms, then stir into bacon and potato mix. Cook for about 5 minutes over medium flame while occasionally stirring.

Grilled smoked sausage go great with this dish

Bandito Burrito

Feeds 8 bandito's for lunch

1 1/2 pounds ground beef
1 16-ounce can refried beans
1/4 cup chili peppers, chopped
1 small onion, chopped
8 tortillas, (burrito size)
hot taco sauce

Break beef up in 12 inch deep skillet, salt and pepper to taste. Add onion and cook over medium flame until beef is done; drain off excess fat. Stir in refried beans and chili peppers. Cook over medium flame while stirring, until hot. Lower heat to warm and stir.

Place 1/8 portion of burrito mix on left side of tortilla. Flap short side of tortilla over mix and roll up like a cigar. Pat burrito semi-flat, using hand. Dip fingers into water and rub over ends of burrito. Pinch one of the ends together, then roll up. Repeat process to other end.

OPTIONS: Top with taco sauce or salsa. Melted cheese works wonders for a topping also. Tortillas can be warmed up in a skillet or on a griddle.

Mountain Fried Macaroni

Feeds 4 as side dish

1 package macaroni & cheese
margarine or butter
ketchup

Prepare macaroni & cheese as directed on package. After meal is prepared, refrigerate overnight in closed container.

Heat 12 inch skillet over medium flame. Add a healthy supply of margarine, so it covers the whole bottom of the pan in skillet. Spread Macaroni & Cheese evenly and flat as possible in skillet. Macaroni & cheese may need to be chopped up a little bit while being heated. (Try not to chop noodles in half.) A spatula or fork works good for this deed.

Fry macaroni & cheese 10–15 minutes over medium flame while chopping and turning noodles with spatula. When noodles finally break up or fall apart from one-another, cook about 3–5 minutes per side before turning. Noodles will be a crisp, golden brown when done.

Top with ketchup, salsa or Tabasco®.

These grits are so good, you'll be lucky to feed 4 as a side dish.

Trout 'N Bacon Breakfast

trout (rainbow, brook, cutthroat, or brown)
bacon
garlic powder
lemon pepper

Clean fish—cut off head, tail, and fins, then rinse with cold water. (Rainbow trout need to be scaled also.)

Cook bacon until done; place on paper towel to drain.

Sprinkle trout inside and out with spices. Place fish in hot bacon fat and cook about 10 minutes while occasionally turning. Trout should flake off with a fork when done.

"Tis better to be lost in the woods,
than found in the city."

Hush Puppies

Feeds 6 as side dish

1 1/2 cups yellow corn meal
1/2 cup all-purpose flour
2 teaspoons baking powder
1/8 teaspoon black pepper
1 tablespoon onion powder
3/4 cup milk
1 egg, beaten

Beat egg and milk; add to remaining ingredients and stir until batter is smooth.

Heat vegetable oil (1/4 inch deep) in 12 inch skillet over medium flame. Drop rounded teaspoons of batter into hot oil and fry about 3 minutes per side until golden brown; turn only once. Place on paper towels to drain. Dip spoon in cold water before each addition. Makes 2 dozen.

Hush Puppies have said to got their name when hunters dropped morsels of corn-cake batter into frying fat, then tossed the cooked portions to the nosy, begging dogs, commanding, "Hush Puppies."

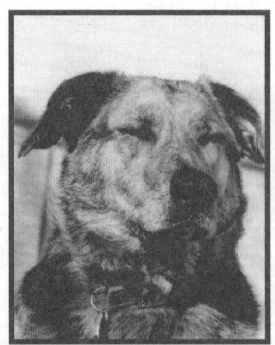

Mmmm, tastes delicious!

Changing of the Seasons

Exploring the wilderness
is so much fun.
It really don't matter
when it's done.
Winter yields a snowy,
frozen mass.
Glacials are formed,
but not to last.
Spring melts down these
icy towers.
Rain patters about to
water the flowers.
Summer brings warm days
with cool nights.
Making camping
a special delight.
Fall weather seems
to come and go.
Though, putting on
a colorful show.
Frosted flurries start to
fly again.
Turning the wilderness
into a winter wonderland.

by Brad Probst

Chapter 2

Griddle Cooking

Breakfast is the main purpose for a griddle. Ordinarily, large quantities of eggs, bacon, sausage and pancakes will be prepared on a griddle for 4 or more people. Griddles come in many sizes, shapes and forms. A griddle 12 x 20 inches is the most common size and fits perfect on any two burner stove. Smaller griddles are available, but most will use a skillet for the intimate couple. Larger griddles are made for campfire units and bigger congregations.

Campfire griddles are easy to use and simple to clean— provided you are equipped with a campfire grill. A campfire grill has four metal legs which provides a sturdy foundation and a level position.

Make sure griddle is heated with cooking oil, margarine or bacon fat before preparing any meals. Cook over reasonable heat (don't scorch food). After food is served, pour water over griddle, then wipe off with paper towels or dish rag. Sounds too easy to be true? It's not!

Breakfast is Brewing

Coffee is a perk'in,
the scent drifts through the air.
Flapjacks are buttered,
while being stacked with care.
Bacon and sausage,
now sizzle on the griddle.
Eggs are scrambled,
but some have been pickled.
If all these vittles have
made you hungry at last.
Pick up your plate,
because it's time for breakfast.

Hillbilly Hash

Feeds 4 for breakfast

1 pound ground beef, chopped
1 15 ounce can whole potatoes, chopped
1 medium onion, chopped
vegetable oil

Cook beef on griddle over medium flame, until done.

Mix potatoes and onions with beef, salt and pepper
 to taste.

Spread hash mix evenly on griddle and cook 10–15
minutes while occasionally stirring. Potatoes should be
brown when done.

OPTION: Sprinkle lightly with red pepper for a more
robust flavor.

Scrambled Eggs

Feeds 4 for breakfast

12 eggs, whipped
2/3 cup milk
butter

Mix eggs with milk and whip with a fork. Heat butter on griddle over medium flame, until butter starts to brown. Poor eggs over butter while using spatula to block eggs from spreading. Lightly salt and pepper eggs. Once eggs have set up, gradually turn eggs over, allowing uncooked portions to settle. Stir and chop moderately with spatula, until eggs have thickened but are still moist. Lightly salt and pepper to taste. If bacon fat is used instead of butter, salt is no longer needed.

French Toast

2 large eggs, whipped
1 cup milk
2 tablespoons sugar
6 slices, Texas bread
cinnamon spice

Take 6 slices of thick bread and set out to dry for about 3 hours. Mix eggs, milk and sugar together and whip with a fork, until uniformed in color. Butter both sides of bread and dip in batter. Place bread on medium hot griddle and sprinkle with cinnamon to taste. Cook 1–2 minutes per side, or until golden brown. Serve with a pat of butter on each piece, then top with powdered sugar or syrup.

Ranch House Omelet

Feeds 4 for breakfast

12 large eggs, whipped
1 1/3 cup cheese, shredded
8 green onions, sliced
1 4-ounce can sliced mushrooms
1 cup milk
butter

Mix eggs and milk together with a dash of salt and pepper, then whip with a fork.

Heat 2 tablespoons butter on griddle over medium flame, making sure bottom of pan is saturated with butter. When butter begins to brown, pour 1/4 of the egg mix on to griddle and stir quickly with a fork. Let stand for a couple of minutes, then add 1/4 of the remaining ingredients while spreading it from one end to the other on the omelet. Fold egg over ingredients and cook for about 30 seconds. Turn omelet over on other side and cook 1 minute, or until cheese has melted.

NOTE: Using jalapeno salsa as a topping, will really please the ranch hands.

Chapter 3

Foil Dinners

Foil dinners are most popular among backpackers, campers and even the backyard barbecue. Backpackers usually wrap beef and raw vegetables in aluminum foil, then bury the packet in hot coals of a fire. Campers and backyard barbecuers use a variety of methods. They most often place the packet on top of red-hot charcoal, gas and barbecue grills, or a smoke cooker.

Before placing food in foil, it's a good idea to rub foil with butter to prevent ingredients from sticking. Seasonings are usually sprinkled on the food before wrapping, except when subject is frozen. Then spices need to be applied after meal has thawed. If chopped vegetables are used, add margarine for flavor. Margarine from a plastic squeeze bottle works best as it can be spread around evenly over the edibles. Do not use margarine on meat products, except for fish and poultry.

After wrapping food in foil, wrap at least 2 more times if packet is going to be buried. This will prevent scorching of food, or holes caused by burning cinder. If this method is used, make sure you have a hot, thick bed of coals. I usually build a small fire on top the coals, while the dinner is cooking.

Aluminum foil comes in different widths. Choose a size accordingly to the bulk of your meal. Foil is also recognized in various different weights. Heavy-duty foil is the most appropriate weight for foil dinners. Thinner foil can be used, but then food has to be wrapped several more times, or risk the possibility of tearing.

Side Dishes

CORN ON THE COB: Roll foil around the cob at least twice, then flap ends over to seal. Cook on top of hot coals, or gas grill for 15 to 20 minutes; occasionally turning.

BAKED POTATO: Wrap foil around potato at least twice, then flap ends over to seal. Bury in hot coals for 45 to 60 minutes, depending on size of potato.

ACORN SQUASH: Cut squash in half and scoop out seeds. Wrap foil around halves at least two times, then bury in hot coals for 60 to 80 minutes, depending on size of squash. Lots of butter and a sprinkle of salt are recommended.

MUSHROOMS: 1/2 pound fresh mushrooms. Slice mushrooms in half, then place on buttered foil and season with salt and pepper. Wrap mushrooms in heavy-duty foil and place packet directly on hot coals for about 5 minutes on each side.

Chicken Cordon Bleu

Feeds 6 as dinner

6 chicken breast
6 pieces, sliced ham
6 thin pieces, Swiss cheese, cut into strips
6 strips, bacon

Rinse chicken in cold water; pat dry.

Skin and bone chicken breast, then beat flat using meat mallet. Place one slice ham and strips of cheese over each breast. Roll ham and cheese up in chicken, then tuck and press ends in to seal. Wrap a strip of bacon around each chicken and pierce with toothpicks on both sides to secure. Clip ends off toothpicks and wrap chicken up in heavy-duty foil.

Place chicken on rack, 2–3 inches above hot coals or charcoal. Cook 15–20 minutes on each side; depending on how thick the chicken is.

TIPS: This is a good one to prepare at home, then put on ice before going camping or whatever.

Backpacker's Buffet

Feeds 1 hungry backpacker

1 steak, or 1/2 pound ground beef
2 strips bacon, cut into squares if beef is used
2 thin slices, onion (dice with beef)
1/2 15-ounce can whole potatoes,
    cut into bite-size pieces
1/2 14-oounce can cut green beans, or carrots,
    drained

Wrap steak, bacon and onion in heavy-duty aluminum foil, forming a packet. Wrap potatoes and green beans in another packet with a pat of butter. Place packet with steak on hot coals 15–20 minutes. Turn steak over after 10 minutes and cook for the remaining time. Bury packet with potatoes and green beans in hot coals 5–10 minutes. Make sure food is wrapped at least two times to prevent leakage or tearing. Remember to season food with your favorite spices before cooking.

TIPS: If dinner is prepared at home, it's a good idea to freeze the steak and place both packets in separately sealed plastic bags. Frozen steak prevents food from spoiling on long journeys, and plastic bags keep juices such as blood and butter from running all over everything.

NOTE: After a long strenuous hike, these basic food groups will replace the protein and vitamins lost while endeavoring a vigorous trek.

"Nothing is opened more often than
a can of worms."

Cajun Foiled Fish

fresh Trout Fillets
margarine or butter
cajun spice and lemon pepper

Rinse fillets in cold water; drain on paper towel.

Sprinkle cajun spice and lemon pepper quite heavily over trout fillets. Put two fillets together with a pat of margarine pressed in the middle. Wrap in heavy-duty aluminum foil. Place wrapped fish directly on top of hot coals, or on rack of covered gas grill. Cook while occasionally turning 15–30 minutes, depending on thickness of fillets.

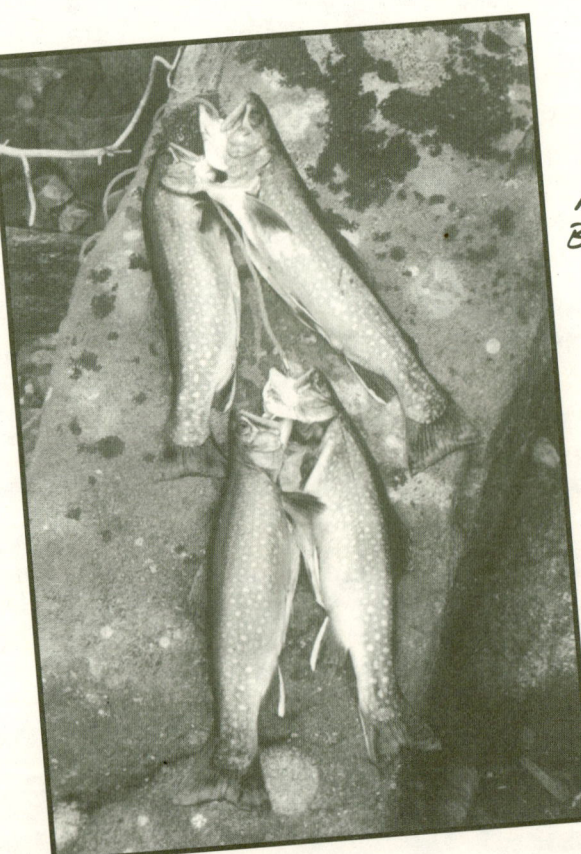

High Uinta
Mountains
Brook Trout

Hobo Dinner

Feeds 2 to 4 as dinner

2 red potatoes, cut into bite-size pieces
1–2 medium heads cauliflower, cut into chunks
1–2 medium heads broccoli, cut into chunks
4 carrots, sliced into 1/4 inch pieces
10 mushrooms, cut into quarters
1 medium yellow onion, chopped
1 medium red onion, chopped
margarine, (squeeze bottle)

Rinse vegetables in cold water; pat dry.

Place all ingredients on heavy-duty aluminum foil and mix. Squirt margarine all over the top of vegetables, then season with your favorite spice. Garlic salt and black pepper work great. Wrap food with foil at least 2 times, forming a packet. Dig out a hole of coals from a fire and bury in coals for about 45 minutes, or until vegetables are tender.

OPTION: Can also be cooked on a covered gas or charcoal grill for 45–60 minutes over medium heat. Make sure you turn packet over after 25 minutes of cooking.

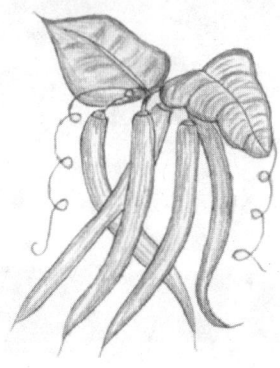

Chapter 4

Grilling & Barbecuing

Campfire grills are designed to cook a variety of meals. They can be applied to cook steaks, hamburgers, pork, poultry, fish, or just to keep things warm such as coffee and stuff. Also, a campfire grill is a necessity when cooking with a griddle. Campfire grills are accommodated with four metal legs which maintains a level position for cooking with a griddle over a campfire.

Temperatures outside may vary, due to wind or cloudy conditions. Check the torridity of flames or charcoal to make sure an even flow of heat is maintained. All foods will need to be cooked longer if cooler temperatures or wind is a factor.

Some campgrounds come with a campfire grill already attached to the campsite. I wouldn't touch these with a 10 foot pole! You never know what kind of plastics or chemicals someone has burned there previously. These substances can leave a real nasty flavor on your food, not to mention serious health problems. Even though, campground grills can be sterilized by the heat of a hot fire. It's just the thought of the matter - how someone might of extinguished the flames in the past. Think about it!

Bratwurst & Sausage

Bratwurst

Bratwurst is about the most easiest and tasty thing there is to cook. Just cook the brats on a gas or charcoal grill, over a medium flame, turn every couple of minutes until the brats are evenly brown and almost blackened in color on all sides. This should take about 20 minutes on a gas grill, and 25 to 30 minutes with charcoal. Brats drip flammable grease, so keep your heat on medium or low, and watch for flare-ups.

Most brats are curved in shape and won't lay on the grill just right to brown all sides. It can be easily done by placing the brats parallel and in between the bars of the grill, or placing the other brats side by side, to hold one another up. Brats are excellent served up with spaghetti and cabbage. Oh, and of course beer.

PRE-COOKED SAUSAGE

Precooked Sausage can be cooked on about anything, even a stick. While backpacking, one of my adored activities is sitting by a fire, roasting smoked sausage for a late-night treat. It puts me in a state of tranquility while feeding my face as well. All you need to do, is find a long forked tree branch and cut off the two branches about 5 inches from the junction. With a knife, shave off the bark of the fork part and make two pointed ends. Stick the fork into the side of the sausage and rotate the sausage 2 to 4 inches above the flames for about 10 minutes, or until sausage begins to split. Sausage should be dark brown and almost black when done. OK, earlier in this chapter it said not to puncture your meat with a fork. However, on certain occasions rules must be broken to accommodate the mood.

Barbecuing Chicken

Real barbecued chicken starts with marinating the chicken first! Rinse chicken, pat dry. Place chicken in a large freezer bag, or sealed in a deep dish with your favorite marinade sauce. Refrigerate overnight while occasionally turning. Marinade sauce can also be used for basting when barbecuing, or as a dipping sauce. Just make sure to boil the sauce for at least 1 minute to kill any bacteria left over from the chicken. Most people decide to skip the marinading process and baste the chicken with barbecue sauce during the last stages of cooking. This is fine. After all, this publication of Campfire Cooking is supposed to be gourmet achieved with ease.

Barbecued Chicken Breast

Rinse chicken; pat dry. Brush a lavish supply of vegetable oil on chicken. Lightly salt and pepper both sides of breast. Place chicken breast bone-side down on cooking rack, 4–6 inches above hot coals or charcoal. Cook for about 20 minutes, then turn over to meat side and cook 8 to 9 minutes. Turn chicken back over to bone-side and cook for another 19 minutes. (If cooking time continues longer than specified, the meat will tend to dry out and be not as juicy). Baste with barbecue sauce a couple of times during the last 10 minutes of cooking. Do not baste with barbecue sauce beforehand. If sauces containing sugar, fruit or tomatoes are used before the last stages of cooking, the sauce will caramelize and burn the outside of the meat.

Skinless Chicken: Skin keeps the chicken from drying out while cooking. So, instead of using barbecue sauce, baste with margarine or butter every 5 minutes from the start. This adds moisture and prevents chicken from drying out.

NOTE: Placing dry, wood flavoring chips or chunks directly on top of hot coals, adds a unique robust flavor to the chicken.

Grilled Fish

When cooking most meats it is recommended to cook over high heat. Fish is no exception. High heat is a necessity for great taste and easy cooking. All that needs to be done, is to spray racks with cooking oil, season fish, heat grill and place fish on rack. About the only hard thing to do is, cleaning or filleting the fish. But then, you can buy them at the super market already prepared that way. However, it will cost you big bucks. $$$$

Fish Fillets

Cooking fillets on a grill is rather simple. Most fillets are cooked about 3 minutes on one side, turned over and cooked 3 minutes on the other, then turned over for a final time to cook 4 more minutes. If temperatures outside are below 75 degrees, or the wind is a factor, fillets will need to be cooked longer. An additional 5 minutes on the opposing side should do the trick. Fillets are done when the meat flakes apart with a fork.

Recommended Fillets

Trout- Rainbow, Cutthroat, Brook and Brown

Steelhead

Salmon

Steaks & Hamburgers

Heat grill over hot flame, before cooking steaks or hamburgers. Place meat on grill and let juices rise to the top of meat. (Do not let juices puddle on top). If juices are allowed to seep out of the meat, the steaks or hamburgers will be dry and tough. Turn meat over every couple of minutes, and permit flames to sear the beef. The searing process will cauterize the outside of the meat, trapping the juices inside. By turning the meat over 3 times using this method, beef should be done medium rare. 5 turns will cook beef medium, and 7 turns should be well done; depending on thickness of meat.

SEASONING: Spices should be placed on meat before cooking, except for salt. Intense heat draws the flavor of the spices through the meat, adding a robust flavor. Salt tends to toughen the meat while cooking. Therefore, if salt is utilized, it is best to sprinkle it on during the last phase of cooking. Some people will work the spices into the meat with a fork. If this method is used, try not to puncher the meat to deep. Holes in the meat will let the juices run out, and the meat will become dry and tough. Also, instead of using a fork to turn the meat, use tongs.

High heat is recommended for these cuts of beef:

Top Round - unless marinated for jerky.

Flank steak	Rib Steak	Rib Eye
Top sirloin	Filet Mignon	New York Strip
Porter House	Tenderloin	T-Bone

HELPFUL HINT: For even cooking, place smaller pieces on edge of grill and thicker pieces in the middle.

Beef Ribs

beef ribs (1 pound per person)
barbecue sauce, homemade, or commercial
1 medium onion, sliced
salt to taste

Cover ribs with cold water in large pot. Add onion and salt; bring to a boil. Cover and simmer 1 hour, or until meat is tender. Place ribs on charcoal grill and brush with barbecue sauce. Cook ribs for about 10–15 minutes, while basting and turning frequently.

Pork Ribs

pork ribs, almost boneless (1 pound per person)
barbecue sauce, homemade, or commercial
salt to taste

Place salted ribs on charcoal grill and cook 35–45 minutes, until pork is tender. Brush with barbecue sauce and turn frequently the last 20 minutes of cooking.

NOTE: Spareribs can be cooked on a gas grill, but cooking time will be a little shorter. Also, turn ribs more often to prevent barbecue sauce from caramelizing.

Shish-ka-bobs

Shish-ka-bobs are one of my favorites. Probably because fingers can be used to eat this dish, and most anything from A to Z can be used. These scrumptious pieces of meat and vegetables can be plucked right off a skewer and into a waiting mouth. Usually lamb is the most common meat utilized, but I've seen others use pork, poultry, venison, beef and even hot dogs. Ordinarily, kebobs are cooked on a charcoal grill. However, if gas is your only feature, they'll do just as well here. Simply turn the skewers more often to prevent veggies from burning.

Lamb Kabobs

Feeds 4 as dinner

1 pound boneless lamb, cut into 1 inch cubes
1 medium green bell pepper,
   cut into 1 inch pieces
1 medium onion, cut into eighths
1 small carton mushrooms, whole or cut in half

Trim excess fat from lamb before cutting into 1 inch cubes. Salt and pepper lamb pieces. Thread or pierce every ingredients on skewer (long skinny stick) in any order as you desire. Usually the onion will be threaded on the skewer next to the lamb so extra flavor will be added to the meat. Place kebobs on hot grill and cook for about 20 minutes, while turning frequently.

NOTE: If wooden skewers are used, soak in water for 30 minutes before use, and make sure food covers all of the skewer so flames don't burn through the wood.

Fragrance of a Barbecue

Ahhh, the aroma of a barbecue
in the great outdoors.
Is about the only thing that will
bring a fisherman back to shore.
That sweet, smokey smell sifting
through the trees.
Will awaken any sleepy nostrils,
pampered by a breeze.
No one will be late when the bell
rings for dinner.
They'll all race to the table to
see who's the winner.
Steaks, hamburgers and hotdogs,
will be all passed around.
Squirrels are looking to salvage,
but no crumbs shall be found.
After the feast is devoured,
everyone pats their belly.
A request comes from the anglers,
" hey, lets cook something smelly."

by Brad Probst

Chapter 5

Smoke Cooking

A smoke cooker can brew up a variety of foods. Everything from breakfast to desserts are a prospect for smoking. There's a bunch of recipes on smoke cooking, but we'll just stick to the basics and use the recipes most often used and easy to fix. Cooking times may vary. Outdoor weather conditions such as temperature, wind and direct sun light will alter the time expected. To ensure the meat is cooked well, a meat thermometer is essential. Insert thermometer into thickest part of the meat and away from any bone or fat for a couple of minutes.

SMOKE FLAVORING WOOD: Smoke flavoring wood adds a unique flavor to the food. Flavors include hickory, mesquite, apple, cherry and pecan. Most any fruit or nut tree will work, but don't use a resin type wood such as pine. Resin wood will leave a repulsive taste on the vittles. Wood comes in different forms such as chunks, chips, sticks and pellets. Wood chunks 4 x 1 inch work best. Soak wood chunks in water at least 1 hour before placing directly on lava rock or charcoal. Wood chips are soaked in water for about 30 minutes, or not at all. Place chips directly on charcoal or in a aluminum container about the size of a tuna can. Another method is to wrap aluminum foil around chips, sticks or pellets and poke several holes in the foil. If an electric smoker is used, don't put wood directly on heating elements.

WATER SMOKING: Most smoke cookers contain a 1 gallon water pan. This pan is usually filled with hot water to evaporate moisture while keeping foods from drying out. In this process, drippings from meat settle in the water, adding extra flavor to the food. Drippings can also be skimmed off the top to make gravy. A full water pan will last about 4–6 hours. For every hour after that, add 1 quart water when needed.

Smoke Cooking Chart

Meat	Weight	Cooking Hours	Temperature of meat thermometer when done
Beef Roast	3–5 lbs.	3–4	140 degrees rare
Lamb Roast	5–7 lbs.	3.5–5	160 degrees medium
Short Ribs	3–6 lbs	2–4	170 degrees well done
Pork Loin Roast	3–7 lbs.	3.5–7	170 degrees well done
Brisket	3–7 lbs.	3–6.5	170 degrees well done
Pork/Beef Ribs	4–10 lbs.	2.5–5	meat pulls away from bone
Pork Chops	6–10 lbs.	2–3	meat pulls away from bone
Ham, fresh	16–18 lbs.	6–8	185 degrees well done
Ham, cooked	all sizes	3–4	140 degrees well done
Chicken, split	full grill	2–2.5	180 degrees leg moves easily in joint
Chicken, whole	2–4 lbs. ea.	2.5–4	180 degrees leg moves easily in joint
Turkey	8–16 lbs.	4–8	185 degrees leg moves easily in joint
Leg of Lamb	5–7 lbs.	3.5–5	140 degrees rare
Venison	3–5 lbs.	3–4	160 degrees medium 170 degrees well done
Fish Fillets	full grill	1.5–2.5	Flakes with a fork
Whole Fish	4–6 lbs.	2–3	Flakes with a fork
Whole Salmon	5–7 lbs.	3.5–6.5	Flakes with a fork
Shrimp, Lobster, Crab Legs, Clams	full grill	1–2	Shrimp pink, Shells open
Cornish Hens	4 hens	2–3	leg moves easily in joint
Small Game Birds	12–16 birds	2–4	leg moves easily in joint
Large Game Birds	5–7 lbs.	4–5	185 degrees well done

Cooking times may vary with altitudes above 3,500 ft. or temperatures below 75° F. or above 85° F.

Smoked Chicken

Feeds 10 as dinner

4 2–3 pounds. whole chicken
vegetable oil
garlic salt, pepper, or seasoning salt

Rinse chicken with cold water; pat dry. Coat chicken inside and out with a lavish supply of oil. Sprinkle seasoning abundantly inside and out.

Fill water pan 3/4 full with hot water. Spray racks with cooking oil; heat smoker.

Place the lightest birds on top rack and the heaviest on bottom. Cook 3–4 hours, or until meat thermometer registers 180 degrees. Legs will move easily in joint when done.

Split Chicken
Follow same procedures listed above, but only cook 2–3 hours.

Marinade
Place chicken in sealed plastic bag with marinade and refrigerate 3–4 hours. Use excess marinade for basting while cooking. Leftover marinade can also be boiled for 1 minute, then served as a dipping sauce.

Tarragon Chicken

Feeds 8 as dinner

2 3–4 pounds. whole chicken
vegetable oil
2 tablespoons lemon juice
2 teaspoons dried tarragon
garlic salt

Rinse chicken with cold water; pat dry. Coat chicken inside and out with vegetable oil. Mix lemon juice and tarragon together and rub into cavity of chicken. Sprinkle outside of chicken with garlic salt.

Fill water pan 3/4 full with hot water and spray racks with cooking oil. Place chicken on racks and smoke cook 3–4 hours, or until meat thermometer reads 180 degrees and legs move easily in joints.

Buffalo Wings

2–3 pounds. chicken wings
1 cup hot pepper sauce
garlic salt, onion powder, and pepper

Rinse chicken; pat dry. Marinade chicken wings in hot pepper sauce for 30 minutes, then sprinkle spices on wings.

Fill water pan 3/4 full with hot water and spray racks with cooking oil. Heat smoker and smoke cook 1–2 hours, basting every half hour with hot pepper sauce. Hot pepper sauce can also be heated and used for dipping. Feeds 4 as dinner.

Wine O' Ham

Feeds 6 to 8 as dinner

1 4–5 pound precooked ham
2 cups red wine

Puncture ham in several places with meat fork. Place ham in deep glass bowl and marinate with wine 2–3 hours while frequently turning.

Fill water pan 1/2 full with hot water. Place ham on cooking rack and smoke cook 3–4 hours, or until meat thermometer reads 140 degrees. Baste with wine periodically while cooking.

Smoked Fresh Ham

1 15–18 pound fresh ham
1 cup brown sugar
1 cup maple syrup
1 cup wine vinegar

Cut ham across top several times about 1/2 inch deep. Mix sugar, syrup and vinegar, then bring to a boil. Place ham in deep bowl and pour mixture over ham. Cover and refrigerate overnight.

Fill water pan full with hot water. (may need to add water during cooking process). Baste ham with mixture and place on cooking rack. Smoke cook 6–8 hours, or until meat thermometer reads 185 degrees. Baste ham a couple of times while cooking. Cook remaining sauce down until thickened; serve with ham.

Hoedown Halibut

Feeds 8 as dinner

4 2-pound halibut steaks
lemon juice
garlic salt and black pepper

Let the party begin... You can smoke cook this one, join the festivities, and no one will even know your cooking up a feast. Just sprinkle the halibut with lemon juice, garlic salt and pepper. Then slap the steaks on the cooking racks, and smoke cook 1–2 hours. Depending on size and quantity. Tartar sauce makes a great topping.

Smoked Shrimp

Feeds 20 to 30 as appetizers

3 pounds large or jumbo shrimp (in shells)
1 1/2 sticks butter
1 1/2 tablespoons black pepper

Wash shrimp in colander. Melt butter and pour in large baking dish. Add shrimp and toss in butter to coat.

Fill water pan 3/4 full with hot water. Place baking dish on cooking rack and smoke cook for 1 hour. Stir once while cooking and after removing from smoker.

Succulent Salmon

Feeds 8 as dinner

4 salmon fillets (about 1 inch thick)
butter, melted
lemon juice
seasoned salt and dill

Rinse fillets in cold water. Mix equal parts butter and lemon juice, then brush mixture on both sides of fillets. Sprinkle with seasoned salt and dill.

Fill water pan 3/4 full with hot water. Place fillets on cooking racks and smoke cook 2 to 2 1/2 hours. Fish should be white in color, and flake with a fork when done.

Cajun Steelhead

Feeds 8 as dinner

4 steelhead fillets
cajun spice

Sprinkle cajun spice on opposite side of skin on fillet. Fill water pan 1/2 full with hot water. Place fillet, skin side down on cooking rack. Smoke cook 1 hour, turn fillet over and peel off skin. Sprinkle with cajun spice and cook another 1–2 hours; depending on size.

Beef Jerky

2 pounds top round steak
1/3 cup soy sauce
salt and pepper

Trim away all fat from steak and don't use pieces with gristle. Cut meat lengthwise with grain, into strips 1 inch wide and no thicker than 1 inch thick. Place strips in flat dish and pour soy sauce over the top of strips. Marinate for 1/2 hour while turning several times. Place strips on chopping board and sprinkle with salt and pepper quite heavily.

Fill water pan 3/4 full with hot water. Spray cooking racks with cooking oil, then place strips on racks so they have space between each other, and do not overlap. Smoke cook 1–2 hours, depending on quantity of strips. Refrigerate after smoking. Jerky will keep 3–4 weeks, if refrigerated. 5–6 days if not!

TERIYAKI: Just add equal parts teriyaki sauce to soy sauce for marinade.

This is a good one for backpacking, snacks, appetizers, picnics, hunting, fishing and camping.

Chapter 6

Desserts

Not many desserts can be made professionally in the great outdoors. Most after-dinner delights are baked in a oven and require special ingredients not ordinarily used for campfire cooking. So, this book will not dawdle on this subject. Besides, the majority of people buy their desserts at the super market. And that's probably a good idea. After all, who wants to spend all their time cooking over a fire pit. On the other hand, if campfire sweets are your desire, a few easy recipes have been rustled up for those delicious delicacies.

Keep desserts in a cool sealed compartment. To show you what I'm talking about, here's a little story about a friend.

A buddy of mine took off one morning to go deer hunting. On his way, he stopped at a store to pick up a minced meat pie. When he arrived at his destination, he pitched his tent and set up camp. Knowing his food would be to hot in the car, he placed all his vittles in the tent.

Later that day, he decided to go on the afternoon hunt. When he got back to camp, it was to dark to see, and to late to cook supper. So, it was resolved. Eat half the minced meat pie, then go to sleep. It tasted so good, he decided to eat most of the pie and save a little slice for morning.

In the morning, he got up and stared at what was left of his delicious dinner. He was stunned to find out that maggots were engulfed in his tasty treat as well...

S'mores

1 bag large marshmallows
1 box Graham crackers

Here's a great one for a tasty treat, or a good-night snack.

Pierce marshmallow in center with long stick or use a hot dog fork. Rotate marshmallow above flames over campfire, until outside of mallow is golden brown and the inside is nice and gooey. Place marshmallow between two Graham crackers, and eat.

OPTION: Add a small piece of your favorite chocolate bar between the crackers.

Marshmallow Bars

32 large marshmallows
1/4 cup margarine or butter
1/2 teaspoon vanilla
5 cups crispy corn puffs (cereal)

Butter bottom and sides of square pan, 9"x9"x2". Heat marshmallows and butter in 3 quart sauce pan over medium flame, stir constantly until mallows have melted.

Remove from heat and stir in vanilla. Stir half the cereal in at a time, until evenly mixed. Pour evenly into square pan, then chill. Cut pieces into 2"x1" bars and serve.

Crepes

1 1/2 cups flour
1 tablespoon sugar
1/2 teaspoon baking powder
2 cups milk
2 tablespoons butter, melted
2 large eggs
1/2 teaspoon vanilla

Mix sugar, flour and baking powder in medium bowl. Stir in remaining ingredients and whip with fork until smooth. Lightly butter 6 inch skillet, heat over medium flame until butter begins to bubble. Pour 1/4 cup batter into skillet and rotate skillet immediately to form a thin film around bottom. Cook until light brown. Run spatula around edge of crepe, turn over and cook other side until lightly browned. Remove crepe from skillet and place on wax paper. Sprinkle with powdered sugar if desired. Stack crepes on top of one another with wax paper dividing each one. Keep covered. Makes 12 crepes.

Mountain Sunrise

Dawn is a approaching, it's a new day of life.
Gray birds sing, while their puerile ones cry.
A fawn walks delicate upon frozen grass.
A crow bellows from heavens past.
Off in the distance, sounds of trickling streams.
The cool wind whispers as it blows through the trees.
One eye opens, so to impel to stretch.
A thrust of deep breath, the mist will catch.
Warmth from the sun enlightens the ground.
A new day of life, is one to be found.
by Brad Probst

Cinnamon Apples

4 large unpeeled apples, golden delicious or greening
4 tablespoons brown sugar
margarine or butter
ground cinnamon

Core apples to within 1/2 inch of bottom. Peel 1 inch strip of skin around middle of apple to prevent splitting. Place 1 tablespoon sugar, 1 teaspoon butter and 1/8 teaspoon cinnamon in center of each apple. Sprinkle apples with cinnamon.

Cut heavy-duty aluminum foil into sections so foil will wrap around each apple twice. Spread butter over one side of foil and wrap apple up in buttered side. Bury wrapped apples in hot coals from a fire for 30–40 minutes; depending on size of apples.

Mr. Stump

Chapter 7

Marinades

Marinade is a spicy sauce used for soaking meat. Ordinarily, meat such as beef, poultry and pork will be placed in a deep dish, then saturated with sauce for several hours before smoke cooking or barbecuing. During the last stages of the cooking process, meat will be basted or brushed with a marinade or barbecue sauce. In addition, marinades or barbecue sauces can be heated up and used for a dipping sauce after meat is served. If leftover marinades are used for dipping, make sure to boil them for 1 minute. Bacteria such as salmonella are still alive, if not boiled. Also, wash any brushes or dishes in which uncooked food was prepared with, if later used on cooked food. Fish products are usually rubbed with a brine made out of a salt and water solution, or heavily brushed, or fried in butter.

Barbecue sauces are mainly used for the final stages of barbecuing or grilling. Most barbecue sauces contain sugar, fruit or tomatoes. If this sauce is applied before or during the cooking process, the sauce will caramelize and burn the outside of the meat. On the other hand, sauces containing a vinegar or mustard base, can be applied before and during the cooking process.

Chicken skin protects the meat from drying out. Marinades or barbecue sauces is your best bet here. If spices are used, they will do little to season the meat. Skinless chicken should be basted with butter every 5 minutes during the cooking process. Also, all chicken which is going to be grilled or barbecued but not marinated or basted with barbecue sauce until the last stages of cooking, should be brushed heavily with vegetable oil after chicken has been rinsed and before spices are added.

Raspberry Basting Sauce

This is a good one to experiment with. Try it on ham, chicken or whatever.

1 12-ounce jar raspberry preserves
1/2 cup ketchup
1 teaspoon chili powder

Strain preserves through sieve; discard seeds. Stir all ingredients together and bring to a boil. Reduce heat and simmer for 2 minutes. *Makes 2 cups.*

Teriyaki Sauce

Goes great with steak, chicken and beef jerky.

1 cup soy sauce
1 cup sugar
1 clove crushed garlic
1/3 cup green onions, chopped

Heat soy sauce and sugar until sugar dissolves. Remove from heat, add remaining ingredients. *Makes 2 cups.*

Tipsy Maple Sauce

Don't drink all the booze before you make this formula!

1/4 cup bourbon
1/2 cup maple syrup
3/4 cup ketchup
1/4 cup vegetable oil
2 tablespoons cider vinegar

Combine all ingredients and whisk to mix well.
Makes 1 3/4 cups.

Chapter 8

Spices

Spices are my favorite. Unlike marinades, spices can season food without drowning out the flavor of the meat. With just a couple of shakes of this and that, you can control the exact amount of flavoring your palate desires. On the other hand, marinades are the dominate ingredients for smoke cooking and barbecuing.

Use spices after marinades or breading is applied. Marinades and breading will inundate meat already seasoned. If these ingredients are utilized, your better off spicing the meat afterwards. (unless barbecue sauce is used for the last stages of cooking). Then spices are put on the meat before. The aroma of spices are drawn through the food fibers while being cooked. Again, if full flavor is to be obtained from the spices, it's best to put your seasonings on after marinades and breading is employed.

If chicken is left with skin still attached, spices do little flavoring for the meat. The only flavoring that will be possessed, will be the seasoning on the skin. Therefore, marinading or barbecuing are the best options when preparing chicken with skin still intact.

Salt should never be placed on meat before cooking. Unless beef jerky is being processed, salt is better off sprinkled on the meat during the last cooking stage. Salt makes meat rather tough and drys out the meat.

"Tidy campers are welcome with open arms, bears have open arms for sloppy campers."

Mesa Verde Spice

Works wonders on chicken or turkey.

2 tablespoons paprika
1 tablespoon red pepper
1 tablespoon garlic powder
1 tablespoon onion powder
1 tablespoon salt

1 teaspoon black pepper
1 teaspoon white pepper
1 teaspoon thyme
1 teaspoon oregano

Cajun Spice

This hot spice goes great on just about everything.

3 tablespoons paprika
2 tablespoon red pepper
2 tablespoon black pepper

1 tablespoon garlic powder
1 tablespoon onion powder
1 tablespoon salt

Smoky Mountain Spice

Best on beef and pork.

2 tablespoons chili powder
2 tablespoon paprika
2 tablespoon black pepper

2 teaspoons salt
1 teaspoon red pepper

Alamo Spice

Excellent on beef.

1/4 cup salt
1/4 cup pepper

2 tablespoons garlic powder
1 tablespoon red pepper

Campfire Cuisine

Warmed by the fire,
everyone is ready to eat.
The coals are nice and hot,
so let's break out the meat.
Bacon and fish now sizzle
in the skillet.
Potatoes and onions will taste
good with the niblet's.
The baked beans are a bubblin',
They'll make a terrific start.
Hope you don't eat to many,
and let me have my part.
After dinner is served,
we'll all gather by the fire.
Roasting marshmallows,
with a long strand of wire.
Please don't drop gooey mallows
around by the fire or soot.
They're a pain in the butt,
to scrape off my boot.
Well, bedtime is approaching,
we had our late-night treat.
May you leave your socks outside,
so I don't smell your feet.

by Brad Probst

Brad Probst

My, how times have changed. Back in the good old days when grandma waited for grandpa to step down from the throne of the outhouse, coal was unveiled to be a prize commodity for stoking a stove. Now, grandpa awaits grandma's departure from the royal palace of wonders, where high tech appliances promptly cook your food.

It's been a long time since my grandparents passed on. Yet, it seems just like yesterday when I went fishing with grandpa. Throughout the years, many memories of camping still linger in my mind. We would all load up the car and head off to Grand Canyon, Yellowstone, or to a local lake for a swim. Nowadays, mom and dad are reluctant to go camping. They are getting up there in age, and for some reason they don't want to sleep under the stars with spiders and snakes. Then there's my sister Pam. She won't go camping unless four walls and room service accommodates her. On the other hand, my brother Jeff will sleep with spiders, snakes and just about anything to take part in camping or fishing.

One of our favorite escapes is the High Uintas in Utah. Jeff and I have made numerous backpacking trips into this area, and have written top selling books on its wilderness. They are called "High Uintas Backcountry" and "High Uintas Fishing." We have prepared many meals for all these excursions, and only the tastiest recipes are recognized in this book.

Special thanks to Jeff Probst and Richard O'Russa for their accomplished work on the layout and editing.

Brad Probst

Respect the Wilderness

In my opinion, any wilderness area is God's country. Although, God made the earth, He probably didn't have much to do with constructing congested cities and chemical plants. This doesn't mean to disrespect the metropolitan regions. It's just to say, keep God's country pure and pristine as possible. So, pick up your trash, tread lightly, respect wild life, and I guarantee God will reward you for your efforts.